THE GET UP A...

ISI...

*Believe in yourself and all that you are.
Know that there is something inside
you that is greater than any obstacle.*

Christian D. Larson

Published in Ireland by
GET UP AND GO PUBLICATIONS LTD

Unit 7A Cornhill Business Complex, Ballyshannon, Co Donegal, F94 C4AA.
Email: info@getupandgodiary.com
www.getupandgodiary.com

Compiled by the Get Up and Go team
Graphic Design by Rosie Gray
Illustrations: freepik.com
Printed in Ireland by GPS Colour Graphics

2026 BANK AND PUBLIC HOLIDAYS

REPUBLIC OF IRELAND
New Year's Day, 1 January
St. Patricks Day, 17 March
Easter Monday, 6 April
June Bank Holiday, 1 June
October Bank Holiday, 26 October
St Stephen's Day, 26 December*
St Brigid's Day, 2 February
Good Friday, 3 April
May Day Bank Holiday, 4 May
August Bank Holiday, 3 August
Christmas Day, 25 December
Bank Holiday, 28 December*

NORTHERN IRELAND
New Year's Day, 1 January
Good Friday, 3 April
May Day Bank Holiday, 4 May
Orangeman's Holiday, 13 July
Christmas Day, 25 December
Bank Holiday, 28 December*
St. Patricks Day, 17 March
Easter Monday, 6 April
Spring Bank Holiday, 25 May
Summer Bank Holiday, 31 August
Boxing Day, 26 December*

ENGLAND, SCOTLAND AND WALES
New Year's Day, 1 January
Good Friday, 3 April
St George's Day, 23 April
Spring Bank Holiday, 25 May
Late Summer Bank Holiday, 31 August
St Andrews Day, 30 November
Boxing Day, 26 December*
2 January, Scotland
Easter Monday, 6 April
May Bank Holiday, 4 May
Summer Bank Holiday, 3 August
Remembrance Day, 11 November
Christmas Day, 25 December
Bank Holiday, 28 December*

USA
New Year's Day, 1 January
Presidents' Day, 16 February
Independence Day, 3 July?
Columbus Day, 12 October
Thanksgiving Day, 26 November
Martin Luther King Jr. Day, 19 January
Memorial Day, 25 May
Labor Day, 7 September
Veteran's Day, 11 November
Christmas Day' 25 December

CANADA
New Year's Day, 1 January
Commonwealth Day, 9 March
Good Friday, 3 April
Victoria Day, 18 May
Civic Day, 3 August
Thanksgiving Day, 12 October
Christmas Day, 25 December
Bank Holiday, 28 December*
Family Day, 16 February
St. Patricks Day, 17 March
Easter Monday, 6 April
Canada Day, 1 July
Labour Day, 7 September
Remembrance Day, 11 November
Boxing Day, 26 December*

AUSTRALIA HOLIDAYS
New Year's Day, 1 January
Good Friday, 3 April
Anzac Day, 25 April
Boxing Day, 26 December
Australia Day. 26 January
Easter Monday, 6 April
King's Birthday, 8 June
Bank Holiday, 28 December

Get up and go diary for busy women 2026

2026 CALENDAR

January

S	M	T	W	T	F	S
				1	2	3
4	5	6	7	8	9	10
11	12	13	14	15	16	17
18	19	20	21	22	23	24
25	26	27	28	29	30	31

February

S	M	T	W	T	F	S
1	2	3	4	5	6	7
8	9	10	11	12	13	14
15	16	17	18	19	20	21
22	23	24	25	26	27	28

March

S	M	T	W	T	F	S
1	2	3	4	5	6	7
8	9	10	11	12	13	14
15	16	17	18	19	20	21
22	23	24	25	26	27	28
29	30	31				

April

S	M	T	W	T	F	S
			1	2	3	4
5	6	7	8	9	10	11
12	13	14	15	16	17	18
19	20	21	22	23	24	25
26	27	28	29	30		

May

S	M	T	W	T	F	S
					1	2
3	4	5	6	7	8	9
10	11	12	13	14	15	16
17	18	19	20	21	22	23
24	25	26	27	28	29	30
31						

June

S	M	T	W	T	F	S
	1	2	3	4	5	6
7	8	9	10	11	12	13
14	15	16	17	18	19	20
21	22	23	24	25	26	27
28	29	30				

July

S	M	T	W	T	F	S
			1	2	3	4
5	6	7	8	9	10	11
12	13	14	15	16	17	18
19	20	21	22	23	24	25
26	27	28	29	30	31	

August

S	M	T	W	T	F	S
						1
2	3	4	5	6	7	8
9	10	11	12	13	14	15
16	17	18	19	20	21	22
23	24	25	26	27	28	29
30	31					

September

S	M	T	W	T	F	S
		1	2	3	4	5
6	7	8	9	10	11	12
13	14	15	16	17	18	19
20	21	22	23	24	25	26
27	28	29	30			

October

S	M	T	W	T	F	S
				1	2	3
4	5	6	7	8	9	10
11	12	13	14	15	16	17
18	19	20	21	22	23	24
25	26	27	28	29	30	31

November

S	M	T	W	T	F	S
1	2	3	4	5	6	7
8	9	10	11	12	13	14
15	16	17	18	19	20	21
22	23	24	25	26	27	28
29	30					

December

S	M	T	W	T	F	S
		1	2	3	4	5
6	7	8	9	10	11	12
13	14	15	16	17	18	19
20	21	22	23	24	25	26
27	28	29	30	31		

FORGIVE THE PAST - LET IT GO
LIVE THE PRESENT - THE POWER OF NOW
CREATE THE FUTURE - THOUGHTS BECOME THINGS

Dear Reader,

Welcome to the 2026 edition of the Get Up and Go Diary for Busy Women!

Whether you're a first-time user or one of our loyal readers, thank you for choosing this inspirational diary. Whether it's a personal purchase or a thoughtful gift, we hope it fills your days with motivation, insight, and encouragement.

Use your diary as a daily planner or a journaling tool. Journaling helps you reflect, set goals, track progress, and stay focused — a powerful practice for personal growth.

Each purchase makes a difference. A portion of every diary sold supports impactful causes in the developing world through our partnership with **B1G1 – Business for Good** (www.B1G1.com). Our paper is sourced from **FSC-certified suppliers**, ensuring it comes from legal and sustainable forests (https://fsc.org).

We're proud to be accredited for the seventh year running by the All-Ireland Business Foundation as a Best in Class Inspirational Publication (www.AIBF.ie).

To explore our full range, buy additional copies, or subscribe to our newsletter, visit **www.getupandgodiary.com**. Stay connected through our community and enjoy early access to new products and discounts. (See order form page 148).

Follow us online:

- Facebook: The Irish Get Up and Go Diary
- Twitter: @getupandgo1
- Instagram: @getupandgodiaries

Love the diary? Share it with your friends and family!

Best wishes for 2026!

From the team at Get Up and Go Publications Ltd

This diary belongs to: _____

Address:_____

Tel: _____   Email:_____

Emergency Telephone Number: _____

Bucket list for *January*

nges and
xperience
and sett
se it as
r, and m
edly, b
s-believ
ations bu
kes you
caught
comes f
o matte
rogress. Surround y
t you, and never be

HAPPY
NEW YEAR

*A New Year is a chance to start a
new and better life.
Make the most of it!*

January

Be Fearless

If you make only one resolution this year, let it be to live boldly. You control this moment. Rather than cautiously test the water, dive straight into life with free abandon. Imagine the person you want to be and the life you want to live, then simply commit to them. Believe in yourself. Embrace your beauty. Discover your passion. And whatever you do, wherever you go, don't be afraid to make a splash.

The perfect woman, you see is a working woman, not an idler, not a fine lady, but one who uses her hands and her head and her heart for the good of others.

Thomas Hardy

Thursday **01**

The future starts here

Friday **02**

Happiness boosts your immune system

Wolf Moon

Saturday **03**

Try out a new look

Sunday **04**

Focus on the task in hand

Even if you are on the right track, you will get run over if you just sit there.

Will Rogers

January

The secret of genius is to carry the spirit of the child into old age, which means never losing your enthusiasm.

Aldous Huxley

Housework can't kill you, but why take a chance?

Phyllis Diller

Monday **05**

Set yourself a 90-day challenge

Tuesday **06**   Women's little Christmas

Your inner voice is not always your friend

Wednesday **07**

Self-acceptance is cheaper than cosmetic surgery

Thursday 08

Remove should, could and would from your vocabulary

Friday 09

It's ok to change your mind

Saturday 10

Guilt is an unproductive emotion

Sunday 11

*Use your words intentionally –
they have great power*

**It's OK if some people don't like you. Not everyone
has good taste.**

Unknown

**If God wanted us to bend over, he'd put diamonds
on the floor." .**

Joan Rivers

January

Live so that when your children think of fairness, caring and integrity, they think of you.

H. Jackson Brown, Jr.

It is not a lack of love, but a lack of friendship that makes unhappy marriages.

Friedrich Nietzsche

Monday 12

Keep going; you're nearly there

Tuesday 13

Charm is an inexpensive quality

Wednesday 14

Be genuinely interested in others

Thursday **15**

Compassion and kindness go a long away

Friday **16**

Feed the birds. Value does not go unnoticed

Saturday **17**

Effective communication is essential for happiness

New Moon

Sunday **18**

Become competent in your area of interest

There is no exercise better for the heart than reaching down and lifting people up.

John Holmes

It takes a big heart to help shape little minds

January

The most effective way to do it is to do it.

Amelia Earhart

Whoever said that money can't buy happiness, simply didn't know where to go shopping.

Bo Derek

Monday **19**

Get to know yourself

Tuesday **20**

You get stronger with every step

Wednesday **21**

In conflict be fair and generous

Thursday 22

In family life, be completely present

Friday 23

Hold on to your dream, it's yours

Saturday 24

Challenge yourself to step outside your comfort zone

Sunday 25

Expect and accept the unexpected

No person is your friend who demands your silence or denies your right to grow.

Alice Walker

January

A person once asked me, How much money is your life worth?

Then proceeded to offer me €100 million for it but there was a clause. The clause was, I wouldn't wake up tomorrow morning. I replied, you KEEP the €100 million,

How much money is your life worth?

Monday **26**

Be a player not a spectator

Tuesday **27**

Don't react, take time to respond

Wednesday **28**

Start your new healthy breakfast trend

Thursday **29**

Knowing is the enemy of learning

Friday **30**

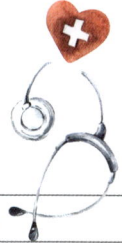

Make that appointment for a health check

Saturday **31**

Be daring / be different

YOUR life and your health are priceless, look after them

A fit, healthy body - that is the best fashion statement.

Jess C. Scott

Quick Lentil Soup

What You Will Need

- 1 Large Onion
- 2½ tsps Fresh Rosemary Leaves (Minced)
- ½ tsp Fine Sea Salt
- ¼ tsp Cracked Black Pepper
- 225g Brown Lentils
- 1.5 Litres of Water

The How-To Part

Chop the onion.

In a large saucepan, bring 1/3 cup water to a boil. Add the onion.

Cook and stir on medium-high until the onion is soft, the water evaporates, and the onion caramelizes to a deep golden brown.

Add the minced rosemary to the onions during the last 30-60 seconds of cooking. Cook and stir to release the oils. Add the salt and pepper, adjust according to taste.

Add the lentils and water. Bring the soup (covered) to a simmer over medium-high heat for about 15 minutes. Reduce heat to low and cook, still covered, for about 15 to 20 minutes longer, or until the lentils are falling apart and the soup is thickened.

When a woman becomes her own best friend, life is easier.

Diane Von Furstenberg

Bucket list for *February*

Don't limit yourself. Many people limit themselves to what they think they can do. You can go as far as your mind lets you. What you believe, remember, you can achieve.

Mary Kay Ash

February

Marriage Box

Many people get married believing a myth that marriage is a beautiful box full of all the things they have longed for: companionship, intimacy, friendship etc. The truth is that marriage, like any relationship, at the start, is an empty box.

You must put something in before you can take anything out. You must put what you want in before you can take what you want out. If you want love in your marriage, there is no love in marriage. Love is in people. And people put love in marriage.

There is no romance in marriage. You have to infuse it into your relationship. A couple must learn the art and form the habit of putting in what they want to get out. Fill your marriage box with kindness, generosity, acceptance, forgiveness and praise, keeping the box full.

If you take out more of your relationship than you put in, very soon your marriage, like the box, will be empty.

Excellence is not a skill it's an attitude.
Ralph Marston

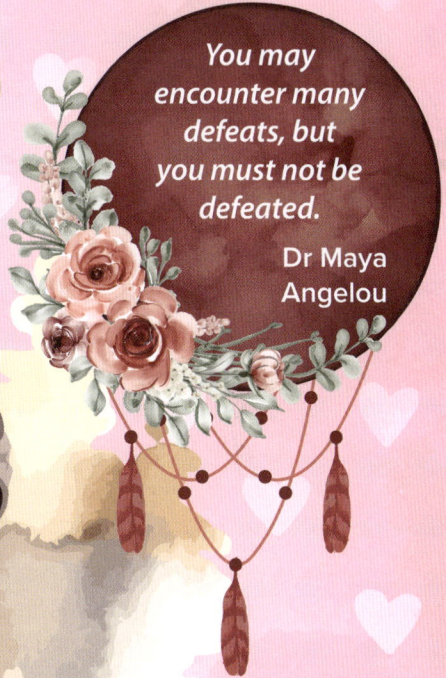

You may encounter many defeats, but you must not be defeated.

Dr Maya Angelou

People skills are the social lubricant of life.
Vanessa Van Edwards

Success isn't about how much money you make; It's about the difference you make in people's lives.
Michelle Obama

Snow Moon	Sunday **01**

Treat yourself to a pampering day

February

A Reporter asks a couple:
How did you manage to stay together for 65 years?

The woman replied:
We were born in a time when if something was broken, we would fix it, not throw it away.

Monday **02**   St Brigid's Day

Learn to delegate

Tuesday **03**

Set yourself a 90-day challenge

Wednesday **04**

Break a habit of a lifetime

Thursday **05**

Work smart – time is money

Friday **06**

Schedule a 'date night'

Saturday **07**

Nurture your spirit

Sunday **08**

Results will always speak for themselves

Empowering women isn't for women, but for the world.

Amy Richards

February

All you need is love. But a little chocolate now and then doesn't hurt.

Charles M. Schulz

There is no greater agony than bearing an untold story inside you.

Maya Angelou

Monday **09**

Celebrate your accomplishments

Tuesday **10**

Be careful not to misinterpret a situation

Wednesday **11**

Stop judging yourself

Thursday **12**

Use 'stress' as fuel for your advantage

Friday **13**

Laugh out loud at least once a day

Happy Valentine's Day

Saturday **14**

One's heart can know what's true

Sunday **15**

Challenge yourself to step outside your comfort zone

Being deeply loved by someone gives you strength, while loving someone deeply gives you courage.

Lao Tau

February

*The sense is clear:
happiness depends on freedom,
and freedom depends on courage.*

Thucydides

*If you can help it. never
shake a hand while
sitting down.*

Anon

Monday 16

Expect and accept the unexpected

Tuesday 17

New Moon
Pancake Tuesday

Take charge

Wednesday 18

Ash Wednesday

Be the person you admire

Thursday **19**

Do it today, you may never be 'ready' enough

Friday **20**

Turn off the (led) light to get a good sleep

Saturday **21**

Happiness boosts your immune system

Sunday **22**

Break big tasks into little tasks

Women and cats will do as they please, and men and dogs should relax and get used to the idea.
                                          Robert Heinlein

Learn to delegate

February

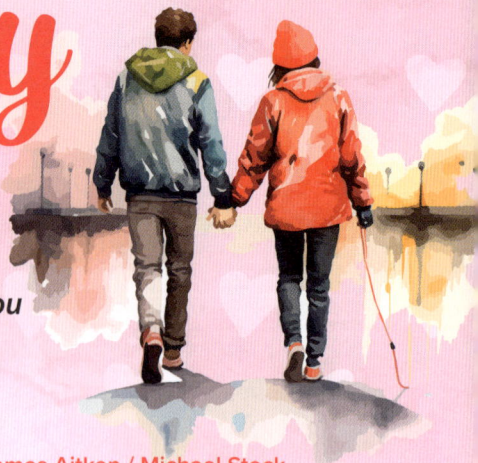

Rick Astley is

Never gonna give you up
Never gonna let you down
Never gonna run around and desert you
Never gonna make you cry
Never gonna say goodbye
Never gonna tell a lie and hurt you

Songwriters: Peter Alan Waterman / Matthew James Aitken / Michael Stock

---

Monday **23**

Prepare well to achieve well

Tuesday **24**

If you want a job done ask a busy person

Wednesday **25**

As you start walking the way appears

Get up and go diary for busy women 2026

Thursday **26**

Every day is a new day to start over

Friday **27**

It's never the wrong time to do the right thing

Saturday **28**

Fix the problem not the blame

I am yours. Don't give myself back to me.

Rumi

The course of true love never did run smooth.
William Shakespeare

Forgiveness is a funny thing. It warms the heart and cools the sting.

William Arthur Ward

Always do the sums, make sure they add up.

Buckwheat Pancakes

Gluten, Dairy, And Refined Sugar Free – From Mama Rae

What You Will Need

- ½ cup buckwheat flour
- ½ teaspoon baking soda
- Pinch of salt
- ½ cup almond milk
- 1 teaspoon apple cider vinegar

The How-To Part

Sift the flour salt and baking powder.

Add the apple cider vinegar to the milk. Gently fold in the milk until the milk is absorbed. Stand in the refrigerator for 15-30 minutes. Heat a non-stick fry-pan and pour batter in. Cook pancakes until bubbles appear on the top and then flip. Drizzle with honey or serve with fresh fruit or berries.

Secrets From Mama Rae's Kitchen

Use the milk you normally use. You can add ½ teaspoon cumin and serve with tomatoes, mushrooms and spinach.

Add a teaspoon of maple syrup/honey and serve with stewed/fresh fruit in season. If you are in a hurry you can leave out the chill 15-30 minutes. These are great served as an accompaniment to a curry dish.

So basically, I don't know what I'm talking about. But maybe I do.

Jenny McCarthy

Love is not affectionate feeling, but a steady wish for the loved person's ultimate good as far as it can be obtained.

C.S. Lewis

If you are trying to be normal you will never know how amazing you can be.

Dr Maya Angelou

The soul is healed by being with children.

Fyodor Dostoyevsky

March

I want to be able to say, that there are four things admirable for a woman to be, at any age! Whether you are four or forty-four or nineteen! It's always wonderful to be elegant, it's always fashionable to have grace, it's always glamorous to be brave, and it's always important to own a delectable perfume! Yes, wearing a beautiful fragrance is in style at any age!

C. JoyBell C

When we least expect it, life sets us a challenge to test our courage and willingness to change; at such a moment, there is no point in pretending that nothing has happened or in saying that we are not yet ready. The challenge will not wait. Life does not look back. A week is more than enough time for us to decide whether or not to accept our destiny.

Paulo Coelho

Sunday **01**

Keep your thinking healthy

Sometimes love means letting go when you want to hold on tighter.

Melissa Marr

March

A History Of Woman's Day

Initially, Woman's day was planned for March 6th. Women took 2 days to get ready. That's how it got postponed to March 8th.

Men's day was also planned...
But as always, they forgot the date!

Monday 02

Your health is your wealth

Tuesday 03   Worm Moon

Give others an opportunity to share their ideas

Wednesday 04

Stay true to your principles

Thursday **05**

Guilt is an unproductive emotion

Friday **06**

Use your words intentionally – they have great power

Saturday **07**

Failing does not make you a failure

Sunday **08**

Happy Women's Day

Tomorrow will present new opportunities

A good woman inspires a man.
A brilliant woman interests him.
A beautiful woman fascinates him.
But a sympathetic woman gets him.

March

*I'm working
On myself,
For myself,
By myself.*

*Love is a two-way street
always under construction.*

Carroll Bryant

Monday 09

Laughter is indeed the best medicine

Tuesday 10   New Moon

Compassion and kindness go a long away

Wednesday 11

Commit to a healthy 'detox'

Thursday **12**

Have faith in yourself and your abilities

Friday **13**

Become competent in your area of interest

Saturday **14**

Get your thoughts in order – write them down

Mother's Day

Sunday **15**

Appreciate the love of your family

A strong woman looks a challenge in the eye and gives it a wink.
Gina Carey

SOMETIMES you win,
SOMETIMES you learn.
John C Maxwell

March

Irish Quote

Irish women are created to be loved not understood.

Hurt me with a truth but never comfort me with a lie.

Erza scarlet

Monday 16

Knowing is the enemy of learning

Tuesday 17 **Happy St Patrick's Day!**

Health is much better than wealth

Wednesday 18

Jump into the river of life and swim downstream

New Moon   Thursday **19**

Hunger finds no fault with cooking

Friday **20**

Don't react, take time to respond

Saturday **21**

Find your favourite place to sit and watch the world go by

Sunday **22**

Count your blessings

You don't drown by falling in the water. You drown by staying there.

Edwin Louis Cole

March

You are a child of the universe, no less than the trees and the stars; you have a right to be here.

Desiderata

Monday **23**

Let go of what you can't control

Tuesday **24**

Listen to your heart

Wednesday **25**

Just breath ... in and out ... in and out ... in and out ...

Thursday **26**

You get stronger with every step

Friday **27**

Life is meant to be abundant in all areas

Saturday **28**

In family life, be completely present

Summer Time Begins

Sunday **29**

Hold on to your dream, it's yours

Make the most of yourself by fanning the tiny, inner sparks of possibility into flames of achievement.

Golda Meir

March

Remember. You will never be at this age again. Please do what makes you happy.

Monday **30**

Have a bath by candlelight

Tuesday **31**   New Moon

Be daring / be different

Why change? Everyone has his own style. When you have found it, you should stick to it.

Audrey Hepburn

Just tell me I can't do it; that'll pretty much guarantee it gets done.

Deidra Mitchell

Irish Tea Cake

What You Will Need

- 1 cup white sugar
- ½ cup butter, softened
- 2 large eggs
- 1 ½ teaspoons vanilla extract
- 1 ¾ cups all-purpose flour
- 2 teaspoons baking powder
- ½ teaspoon salt
- ½ cup milk, or more if needed
- ¼ cup confectioners' sugar for dusting

The How-To Part

1. Preheat the oven to 350 degrees F (175 degrees C). Grease and flour a 9-inch round pan.
2. Cream sugar and butter together in a mixing bowl with an electric mixer until light and fluffy. Beat in eggs, one at a time, mixing until fully incorporated after each addition. Stir in vanilla.
3. Combine flour, baking powder, and salt in a mixing bowl. Stir dry ingredients into wet ingredients alternately with milk, adding 1 to 2 tablespoons more milk if batter is too stiff. Spread batter evenly into the prepared pan.
4. Bake in the preheated oven until a toothpick inserted into the center comes out clean, 30 to 35 minutes. Cool in the pan on a wire rack for 10 minutes.
5. Turn cake out onto a serving plate and cool to room temperature, 20 to 30 minutes. Dust with confectioners' sugar right before serving.

Sometimes what you're looking for comes when you're not looking at all.

Anon

> *Create your own style... let it be unique for yourself and yet identifiable for others.*
>
> Anna Wintour

> *If hard work is the key to success, most people would rather pick the lock.*
>
> Claude McDonald

> *The meaning of things lies not in the thing themselves, but in our attitude towards them.*
>
> Antoine de Saint- Exupery

Bucket list for *April*

Spring will come and so will happiness. Hold on. Life will get warmer.
Anita Krizzan

Don't look at your feet to see if you are doing it right. Just dance.
Anne Lamott

April

Get into good shape, remember round is also a good shape.

If plan 'A' doesn't work the alphabet has 25 more letters.

Claire Cook

Do what you love, and success will follow. Passion is the fuel behind a successful career.

Meg Whitman

Wednesday 01

Stay on purpose and bring purpose to what you do

Pink Moon	Thursday **02**

Happiness is a choice

Good Friday	Friday **03**

Know the power of intention

	Saturday **04**

It's all unfolding according to plan. Relax

Easter Sunday	Sunday **05**

Stay in a state of gratitude

Easter is the only time of year when you can put all your eggs in one basket.

Unknown

April

Having a positive mental attitude is asking how something can be done rather than saying it can't be done.

Bo Bennett

I was smart enough to go through any door that opened.

Joan Rivers

Monday 06

Easter Monday

Make peace with your past

Tuesday 07

Let go of resistance

Wednesday 08

Keep your thoughts and feelings in harmony with your actions

Thursday **09**

Change thoughts of judgement to thoughts of compassion

Friday **10**

Respect your body

Saturday **11**

Children are like sponges – they soak up what they see and hear

Sunday **12**

Remind yourself you are never alone

**You don't have to be the best.
You just have to be the best you.**

Tina Fey

April

You have to have confidence in your ability and then be tough enough to follow through.

Rosalynn Carter

You can never leave footprints that last if you are always walking on tiptoe.

Leymah Gbowee

Monday 13

Do what you know to do

Tuesday 14

Forgiveness, not blame, is the key

Wednesday 15

You are worthy of love

Thursday **16**

Time is a great healer

New Moon   Friday **17**

Affirm yourself with your personal affirmations

Saturday **18**

Change 'I' to 'we' and turn illness to wellness

Sunday **19**

Appreciate your community

The man that says his wife can't take a joke, forgets that she took him.

Oscar Wilde

April

One is never over-dressed or underdressed with a Little Black Dress.

Karl Lagerfeld

Rivers know this: there is no hurry. We shall get there someday.

A.A. Milne

Monday **20**

Get up, dress up and show up

Tuesday **21**

Keep your finances in order

Wednesday **22**

Let people "tell you what to do"

Thursday **23**

Teach people how to treat you by treating them the same

Friday **24**

Happiness is an advantage

Saturday **25**

Challenge your firmly held beliefs

Sunday **26**

Remember where you came from

Style is a reflection of your attitude and your personality.

Shawn Ashmore

April

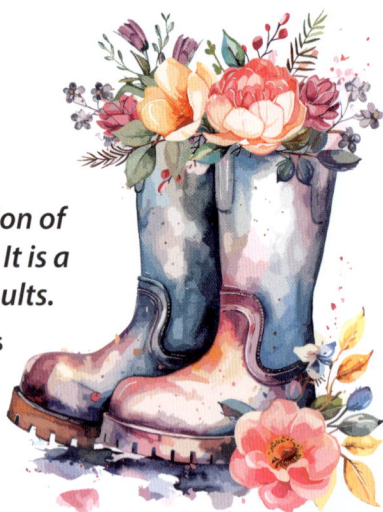

A positive attitude causes a chain reaction of positive thought, events and outcomes. It is a catalyst, and it sparks extraordinary results.

Wade Boggs

A Man's day off is "his day off"
A Woman's day off is time to catch up on housework.

Unknown

Monday 27

Focus your energy on what you need to handle now

Tuesday 28

Your life is in order, manage your moments

Wednesday 29

Tidy your desk or your workspace

Your health is your responsibility, get it checked

If a man says he will do it, he will do it.
There is no need to remind him every six months.
Preeti Shenoy

Find a problem you care about and start solving it. Obviously, you're not going to fix the world's problems by yourself. But you can contribute and make a difference. And that feeling of making a difference is ultimately what's most important for your own happiness and fulfilment.

Anzac Biscuits

Gluten, Dairy and Refined Sugar Free – From Mama Rae

What You Will Need

- 1 ½ cups quinoa flakes
- ¾ cup shredded coconut
- ¼ cup coconut oil
- 2-3 tablespoons maple syrup
- 1 teaspoon vanilla
- ½ teaspoon baking soda

The How-To Part

Turn your oven on to 150 degrees. Process 1 cup of the quinoa flakes, the shredded coconut, and the baking soda until it resembles breadcrumbs. Transfer to a bowl and add the rest of the quinoa flakes. Put all the wet ingredients into a separate bowl and mix before adding to the quinoa, coconut and soda. Stir until mixed evenly. You may want to add some water/milk, teaspoon by teaspoon so the mixture sticks together. Place teaspoonfuls of the mixture on a baking tray (line with baking paper if you wish) and then flatten with a fork. Bake your Anzac biscuits for 20 – 30 minutes, until they are golden brown.

Secrets From Mama Rae's Kitchen

You could use any other flakes, eg. oats or a mix of them. Try other oils instead of coconut. Macadamia oil is yummy but expensive. I have added ½ cup currants to this recipe or you could add ½ cup of slivered almonds for something different. They are a little bit fiddly to get into balls and flatten, but worth it. I sometimes use ginger syrup as the sweetener, for added flavour.

The greatest happiness of life is the conviction that we are loved; loved for ourselves, or rather, loved in spite of ourselves.

Victor Hugo

Bucket list for *May*

Never limit yourself because of others' limited imagination; never limit others because of your own limited imagination.

Mae Jeminson

May

Don't be into trends. Don't make fashion own you, but you decide what you are, what you want to express by the way you dress and the way to live.

Gianni Versace

The ordinary focus on what they're getting. The extraordinary think about who they are becoming.

Unknown

We must have perseverance and above all confidence in ourselves. We must believe that we are gifted for something.

Marie Curie

Find three hobbies you love:
One to make you money
One to keep you in good shape
And one that allows you to be creative.

Flower Moon	Friday **01**

It takes energy to overcome inertia. Give yourself a kick start

	Saturday **02**

Your most valuable resource is your social support – reach out

	Sunday **03**

Modern life guarantees distraction – stay focused

Love is a fire. But whether it is going to warm your hearth or burn down your house, you can never tell.

Joan Crawford

May

Your time is important, so is everyone else's, don't be late.

I am not a product of my circumstances; I am a product of my decisions.

Stephen Covey

Monday **04**	May Day

Be at peace with yourself and others

Tuesday **05**	

Procrastination is not always bad ... timing is everything

Wednesday **06**	

Boundaries get blurred over time – keep redrawing the lines

Thursday **07**

There is time for everything – just not all at once

Friday **08**

There are many answers to a single question

Saturday **09**

Choose the healthy option

Sunday **10**

In business find a mentor

A healthy outside starts from the inside.

Robert Ulrich

May

There is no force more powerful than a woman determined to rise.

W.E.B. Dubois

You know all those things you've always wanted to do? You should go and do them.

Andy Andrews

Monday **11**

Listen to the advice of friends and loved ones

Tuesday **12**

Reignite your passion

Wednesday **13**

Don't deny yourself the right to a great life

Thursday **14**

Prepare well to achieve well

Friday **15**

We can all learn from children

New Moon

Saturday **16**

Keep it simple

Sunday **17**

Plan a holiday

Who ever said 'diamonds are a girl's best friend', never owned a dog!

Anon

May

Girls should never be afraid to be smart.

Emma Watson

Monday **18**

Let go of doubt and fear

Tuesday **19**

Get enough sleep

Wednesday **20**

Stay connected with your parents if you can

Thursday 21

Worrying is misuse of imagination

Friday 22

Allocate time for family and friends

Saturday 23

Create your home as the place you love to come home to

Sunday 24

Do what you say you will do

The more you know of your history, the more liberated you are.

Dr Maya Angelou

May

Beauty is about perception, not about make-up. I think the beginning of all beauty is knowing and liking oneself. You can't put on make-up, or dress yourself, or do your hair with any sort of fun or joy if you're doing it from a position of correction.

Kevyn Aucoin

Monday **25**

Show up on time

Tuesday **26**

Don't worry about what you cannot control

Wednesday **27**

It is enough to be who you are

Thursday **28**

Never speak little of yourself

Friday **29**

Your best is always good enough

Saturday **30**

Stumbling is not falling

Full Blue Moon

Sunday **31**

Forget the mistakes of the past

Life is hard. After all, it kills you.
Katherine Hepburn

Old ways won't open new doors.
Anonymous

Tasty Vegetarian Quiche

What You Will Need

- 2 tablespoons Extra-Virgin Olive Oil
- 8 oz Fresh Mixed Wild Mushrooms (sliced)
- 1 ½ cups Sweet Onion (thinly sliced)
- 1 tablespoon Garlic (thinly sliced)
- 5 ounces Fresh Baby Spinach
  (about 8 cups, coarsely chopped)
- 6 Large Eggs
- ¼ cup Whole Milk
- ¼ cup Half-And-Half
- 1 tablespoon Dijon Mustard
- 1 tablespoon Fresh Thyme Leaves
  (plus more for garnish)
- ¼ teaspoon Salt
- ¼ teaspoon Ground Pepper
- 1 ½ cups Gruyere Cheese (shredded)

The How-To Part

1. Preheat oven to 375 degrees F. Coat a 9-inch pie pan with cooking spray; set aside.

2. Heat oil in a large nonstick frying pan over medium-high heat; swirl to coat the pan. Add mushrooms; cook, stirring occasionally, until browned and tender, about 8 minutes. Add onion and garlic; cook, stirring often, until softened and tender, about 5 minutes. Add spinach; cook, tossing constantly, until wilted, 1 to 2 minutes. Remove from heat.

3. Whisk eggs, milk, half-and-half, mustard, thyme, salt and pepper in a medium bowl. Fold in the mushroom mixture and cheese. Spoon into the prepared pie pan. Bake until set and golden brown, about 30 minutes. Let stand for 10 minutes; slice. Garnish with thyme and serve. (Serves 6). Serve with a light salad for lunch.

Bucket list for *June*

nges and
xperience
and sett
se it as
r, and m
edly, b
s-believ
tions bu
kes you
caught
comes f
o matte
progress. Surround y
t you, and never be

*I was smart enough to go
through any door that opened.*

Joan Rivers

*A negative mind will never give
you a positive life.*

Ziad K. Abdelnour

June

You are where you are in life because of what you believe is possible for yourself.

Oprah Winfrey

Sometimes the right path is not the easiest one.

Pocahontas

Monday **01**   June Bank Holiday

See the beauty in yourself

Tuesday **02**

Life is a school, and we are all here to learn

Wednesday **03**

Be willing to forgive

Thursday 04

Anyone can hold the helm when the sea is calm

Friday 05

Take the time to get a medical check up

Saturday 06

Avoid buying what you do not need just because you think it's a bargain

Sunday 07

You can deal with any situation

I've been absolutely terrified every moment of my life, and I've never let it keep me from doing a single thing that I wanted to do.
Georgia O'Keeffe

June

You can never leave footprints that last if you are always walking on tiptoe.

Leymah Gbowee

Monday 08

Do the things you have always wanted to do

Tuesday 09

It's ok to have quiet days

Wednesday 10

Change your thoughts and you change your world

Thursday **11**

Being an optimist is good for your health

Friday **12**

Your health is your wealth; guard it

Saturday **13**

No problem is insurmountable

Sunday **14**

Daily exercise is conducive to wellbeing

If you reveal your secrets to the wind, you should not blame the wind for revealing them to the trees.

Kahlil Gibran

June

The will to win, the desire to succeed, the urge to reach your full potential... these are the keys that will unlock the door to personal excellence.

Confucius

Monday **15**	New Moon

Remember those who inspired you, and why

Tuesday **16**	

Being happy is a way of being wise

Wednesday **17**	

Create your home as a haven of peace and a piece of heaven

Thursday **18**

Attitude is everything

Friday **19**

The colour of truth is mostly grey

Saturday **20**

Believe in the power of one

Father's Day

Sunday **21**

What you do makes a difference

Angry people want you to see how powerful they are. Loving people want you to see how powerful you are.

Chief Red Eagle

June

Find ecstasy in life; the mere sense of living is joy enough.

Emily Dickinson

People are going to judge you anyway, so you might as well do what you want.

Taylor Swift

Monday **22**

Trust is the foundation of any worthwhile relationship

Tuesday **23**

Choose to see the world through grateful eyes

Wednesday **24**

Speak your mind

Thursday 25

Share your sparkle wherever you are

Friday 26

The future is created, not promised

Saturday 27

Keep your ideals high and raise your standards

Sunday 28

Look forward and ask why not

Don't sit down and wait for the opportunities to come - get up and make them.

Madam C.J. Walker

June

There is no limit to what we, as women, can accomplish.

Michelle Obama

Be careful who you trust, sugar and salt look the same.

Bill Lewis

Monday 29

If you're going through hell, keep going

Tuesday 30   Strawberry Moon

Eating words rarely causes indigestion

When I eventually met Mr. Right, I had no idea that his first name was Always.

Rita Rudner

Sometimes good things fall apart so better things can fall together.

Marilyn Monroe

Healthy Fruit Punch

What You Will Need

- 12 Grapes
- 120 grams Blueberries
- 1 Orange
- ½ Lemon
- ½ Lime
- 400 millilitres Sparkling Water
- 500 millilitres 100% Cranberry Juice
- 12 Cherries
  Mint Leaves (to garnish)

The How-To Part

1. Divide the grapes and blueberries evenly over 2 ice-cube trays. Cover with cold water and place in the freezer for 3-4 hours or overnight until set.
2. Cut the orange, lemon and lime into thin slices and add to a punch bowl or large (1.5-2L capacity) serving jug.
3. Pour over the sparkling water and cranberry juice. Add the fruit ice cubes and cherries, and stir to combine.
4. Serve immediately, garnished with mint leaves. Enjoy!

I believe everything happens for a reason.
People change so you can learn to let go.
Things go wrong so you can appreciate them when they're right.
You believe lies so you can learn to trust no one but yourself
and sometimes good things fall apart so better things
can fall together...

Marilyn Monroe

Nobody notices your pain, but
everyone notices your mistakes.

Unknown

*May the flowers remind us why
the rain was so necessary.*

Xan Oku

When life throws you a rainy day,
play in the puddles.

Winnie the Pooh

Bucket list for *July*

nges and
xperience
and sett
se it as
r, and m
edly, b
s-believ
ations bu
kes you
caught
comes f
o matte
rogress. Surround y
t you, and never be

Life is a series of natural and spontaneous changes. Don't resist them; that only creates sorrow. Let reality be reality. Let things flow naturally forward in whatever way they like.

Lao Tzu

July

It's never too late to start over. If you weren't happy with, yesterday try something different today. Don't stay stuck, do better.

Alex Elle

Wanting to be someone else is a waste of who you are.

Kurt Cobain

Wednesday **01**

Avoid worry; think and plan

Thursday 02

Be at peace with your age

Friday 03

Life is all about chance, choice and change

Saturday 04

Happy is the new rich

Sunday 05

Take care of your body

Your body will be around a lot longer than that expensive handbag. Invest in yourself.

Unknown

F-E-A-R has two meanings: "Forget Everything And Run" or "Face Everything And Rise.

July

If you don't like the road you're walking, start paving another one.
Dolly Parton

When you face your fears, they shrink, and you grow.

Jay Bennett

Monday **06**

You will see it when you believe it

Tuesday **07**

Let the past make you better, not bitter

Wednesday **08**

Keep two days a week worry free, Yesterday and Tomorrow

Thursday **09**

Everyone deserves to be understood

Friday **10**

Differences enrich families

Saturday **11**

Your life is your responsibility

Sunday **12**

Age is no barrier

A successful man is one who makes more money than his wife can spend.
A successful woman is one who can find such a man.

Lana Turner

July

When you accept that failure is a good thing, it can actually be a huge propeller toward success.

Whitney Wolfe Herd

Monday 13

Tidy your cupboards

Tuesday 14   New Moon

Don't be afraid to try something new

Wednesday 15

Let go of negativity

Thursday **16**

Start a new hobby

Friday **17**

Enjoy the outdoors

Saturday **18**

Always try to see the 'big picture'

Sunday **19**

Self-acceptance is the doorway to greatness

Instinct won't carry you through the entire journey. It's what you do in the moments between inspiration.

Cate Blanchett

July

Always remember that you are absolutely unique. Just like everyone else.

Margaret Mead

You are what you do, not what you say you'll do.

Carl Jung

Monday **20**

You will be alright whatever happens

Tuesday **21**

Do something today that you love doing

Wednesday **22**

Creation is the spice of life

Thursday **23**

Look. Listen. Choose. Act

Friday **24**

Good temper oils the wheels of life

Saturday **25**

We all have all the time there is

Sunday **26**

You are the source of your own experience

We are most alive when we're in love.
John Updike

Judge me when you are perfect.
Ziad K. Abdelnour

July

True happiness... is not attained through self-gratification, but through fidelity to a worthy purpose.

Helen Keller

What's coming will come and we will meet it when it does.   **Hagrid**

Monday **27**

Keep your house in order

Tuesday **28**

A good book is a good companion

Wednesday **29**   **Buck Moon**

Invite friends to dinner

	Thursday **30**

Trust your intuition

	Friday **31**

Don't judge people by their relatives

Speedy Bean Chilli

What You Will Need

- *Half a red onion*
- *One chopped carrot and courgette*
- *One cup of frozen peas and corn*
- *One can of red kidney beans (rinsed) and one can of diced tomatoes*
- *Seasonings such as salt, pepper, paprika, chilli powder and cumin*

The How-To Part

1. *In a large saucepan sweat the onion off in some oil, add the carrot and courgette until they are slightly softened. Add the frozen veg, cook for a minute then add the beans, tomatoes and seasoning.*
2. *When all the vegetables are cooked through, serve immediately.*

Bucket list for August

*nges an
xperience
and set
se it as
r, and m
edly, b
s-believ
ations bu
kes you
caught
comes f
o matte
rogress. Surround y
you, and never be

*Dwell on the beauty of life.
Watch the stars and see yourself
running with them.*

Marcus Aurelius

*I love deadlines. I like the whooshing
sound they make as they fly by.*

Douglas Adams

Usually, time takes a flight when we are enjoying ourselves, but we all have got the same amount of time.

60 seconds in 1 minute
3600 seconds in 1 hour
86400 seconds in 1 day
604800 seconds in 1 week
2628002 seconds in 1 month
31.536,000 seconds in 1 year
1 billion seconds in 31.71 years
1 trillion seconds in 31709.80 years

Do not waste 1 second

Saturday 01

Remain warm and approachable

Sunday 02

Spend the afternoon in a garden

Nature has given us all the pieces required to achieve exceptional wellness and health but has left it to us to put these pieces together.

Diane McLaren

August

Love is not about how much you say, 'I love you,' but how much you prove that it's true.
Unknown

Sometimes people feel the rain, others just get wet.
Bob Marley

Monday **03**	August Bank Holiday

Having a sharp tongue can cut your own throat

Tuesday **04**

Be patient with children

Wednesday **05**

Allow extra time to get to where you're going

Thursday **06**

Miracles do happen

Friday **07**

Things don't matter; people do

Saturday **08**

Home is where the heart is

Sunday **09**

You are responsible for your own happiness

There are only three things women need in life: food, water, and compliments. Chris Rock

You are far too smart to be the only thing standing in your way. Jennifer J. Freeman

August

I do business with my heart as much as I do with my head, both personally and professionally.

Ursula Burns

Nobody can go back and start a new beginning, but anyone can start today and make a new ending.

Mary Robinson

Monday 10

For all of us there are turning points in our lives.

Tuesday 11

Recall happy events and re-experience happy memories

Wednesday 12   New Moon

Make and keep promises

Thursday **13**

Don't let the turning world spin you out of control

Friday **14**

Get enough sleep

Saturday **15**

Acknowledge the accomplishments of others

Sunday **16**

Let those who love you help you

Whatever you do, be different. If you're different, you will stand out.
Anita Roddick

Don't live the same life over and over again! Make a change this time. **Rita Mae Brown**

August

A person's favourite sound is their name, so remember it.

Dale Carnegie

Don't be afraid of losing people, but be afraid of losing yourself trying to make everyone happy.

Naguib Mahfouz

Monday 17

Nurture your relationships

Tuesday 18

Life always gives us second chances

Wednesday 19

When in doubt, take courage

Thursday **20**

A family is a strong support network

Friday **21**

Have dinner by candlelight

Saturday **22**

Pay attention to your diet

Sunday **23**

Don't choose to suffer

Too many of us are not living our dreams because we are living our fears.

Les Brow

August

We must have perseverance and above all confidence in ourselves.

Marie Curie

Monday **24**

You are everything to someone

Tuesday **25**

Note any bad habits and plan to correct them

Wednesday **26**

Light a candle in memory of someone you loved and lost

Thursday **27**

Plan a family outing

Sturgeon Moon

Friday **28**

Challenge yourself with a new goal

Saturday **29**

Consider travelling to somewhere you have never been

Sunday **30**

Don't overdose on duty

Everyone has the right to be stupid, but some just abuse the privilege.

Joseph Stalin

August

When you're kind and you treat people with kind, You get treated in kind.

Glen Campbell

Monday **31**

Don't forget about getting your health checked

Snack Balls

Gluten, Dairy, And Refined Sugar Free – From Mama Rae

What You Will Need

8 dates
⅓ cup walnuts
2 tablespoons cacao
⅓ cup coconut
¼ teaspoon cinnamon

The How-To Part

Put all the ingredients into the food processor. Process until the mixture is crumbly and sticky. Roll into balls. Store in a sealed container in the refrigerator.

Secrets From Mama Rae's Kitchen

Substitute any other nuts for the walnuts. Add ¼ cup of chopped dried apricots or cranberries for something different. You can take out the cacao and add a tablespoon of lemon juice. Maybe start with 2 teaspoons, taste and add more little by little. If you want a sweeter bliss ball then add some more dates.

Bucket list for *September*

Too many people spend money they earned. To buy things they don't want. To impress people that they don't like.

Will Rogers

September

Being happy doesn't mean that everything is perfect. Being happy means, everything is perfect just the way it is.
Gerard Way

Forgive all before you go to sleep, you'll be forgiven before you get up.
Lord Krishna

It's not our job to toughen our children to face a cruel and heartless world. It's our job to raise children who will make the world a little less cruel and heartless.
LR Knost

Tuesday **01**
Have a good laugh

Wednesday **02**
If you try, you might; if you don't, you won't

Thursday **03**

Choose your family as they are

Friday **04**

We all have many lessons to learn

Saturday **05**

We each have the best of us at the heart of us

Sunday **06**

Have a guilt free 'do-nothing' day

I hate housework! You make the beds; you wash the dishes and six months later you have to start all over again.

Joan Rivers

September

We need women at all levels, including the top, to change the dynamic, reshape the conversation, to make sure women's voices are heard and heeded, not overlooked and ignored.

Sheryl Sandberg

Monday **07**

Some days are simply perfect

Tuesday **08**

There is a time for everything

Wednesday **09**

Don't jump to conclusions, you many fall

Thursday 10

Ask yourself "is it true, is it fair?"

New Moon   **Friday 11**

Be a supportive friend

Saturday 12

Time never flies faster than one minute/hour at a time

Sunday 13

Knock where the door is open

One of the most courageous decisions you will ever make is to finally let go of whatever is hurting your heart and soul.

Brigitte Nicole

September

There are people who would love to have your bad days.

Susan Sparks

Success does not start at the top; it begins by deciding to get up from the bottom.

Ken Poirot

Monday **14**

Have a conscious positive intention in every situation

Tuesday **15**

Use 'and' more often than 'but'

Wednesday **16**

If you want the fruit, climb the tree

Thursday **17**

Notice the everyday miracles of nature

Friday **18**

Everyone has something unique worth saying

Saturday **19**

Thoughts are seeds of deeds

Sunday **20**

Put your dreams to work for you

Anyone who says he can see through women is missing a lot.

Groucho Marx

September

The thing women have yet to learn is nobody gives you power. You just take it.

Roseanne Barr

With freedom, books, flowers and the moon, who could not be happy?

Oscar Wilde

Monday **21**

Take the initiative

Tuesday **22**

Practice compassion

Wednesday **23**

Be an attentive listener

Thursday **24**

Have a beautiful, inspired day

Friday **25**

Be done with yesterday so it doesn't interfere with today

Full Moon, Harvest Moon   Saturday **26**

When anger rises, think of the consequences

Sunday **27**

*There is nothing to be gained
by putting yourself down*

**I have yet to hear a man ask for advice
on how to combine marriage and a
career.**

Gloria Steinem

September

*Nobody's a natural.
You work hard to
get good and then
work to get better.*

Paul Coffey

Monday 28

Someone values your advice

Tuesday 29

Life is short; make fun of it

Wednesday 30

Wherever you go, go with all your heart

Bucket list for *October*

We are supposed to enjoy the good stuff now, while we can, with the people we love. Life has a funny way of teaching us that lesson over and over again.

Sheena Easton

October

Thoughts on moving on....

First I was dying to finish school and start college
Then I was dying to finish college and start working
Then I was dying for Friday so I could have fun on the weekend
Then I was dying with a hangover
Then I was dying to get married and start a family
Then I was dying for my children to be old enough so I could go back
to work and have a career.
Then I was dying to retire.
Now I am dying, and I have suddenly realised that I forgot to live.

Anon

Thursday 01

Respect yourself and others will respect you

Friday 02

A trade not properly learned is an enemy

Saturday 03

If you can't be a good example, be a horrible warning

Sunday 04

Change is inevitable, learn to embrace it

Until you make peace with who you are you will never be content with what you have.

Doris Mortman

October

For a great night, Go dancing
For a great weekend, Go dancing
For a great week, Go dancing
For a great year, Go dancing
For a great life, Go dancing
For a great indoor hobby, Go dancing
For a great healthy lifestyle,
Go dancing

Monday **05**

Play full out

Tuesday **06**

We build the ladder by which we rise

Wednesday **07**

Only complain to someone who can do something about it

Thursday **08**

There is no 'no' in life

Friday **09**

You must do the thing you think you cannot do

New Moon

Saturday **10**

Stay focused on what you want

Sunday **11**

Be slow to punish

Don't look at your feet to see if you are doing it right. Just dance.
Anne Lamott

October

A little progress each day adds up to big results.

Satya Nani

When looking back doesn't interest you anymore, you're doing something right.

Alf Dunbar

Monday **12**

Start the day with a hearty breakfast

Tuesday **13**

Relax, it's perfect the way it is

Wednesday **14**

Give up any pretence

Thursday **15**

Keep calm and carry on

Friday **16**

Plan a 'feel-good-away-day' with your best friend

Saturday **17**

Be willing to be open to something new

Sunday **18**

Be true to yourself

Always do your best.
What you plant now,
you will harvest later.

Og Mandino

October

*You have within you more love
than you could ever understand.*

Rumi

*I have learned over the years
that when one's mind is made
up, this diminishes fear.*

Rosa Parks

Monday **19**

Stay aligned with your purpose in life

Tuesday **20**

Reignite the creativity of your childhood

Wednesday **21**

Stop doing what doesn't work

Thursday **22**

Engage in lifelong learning

Friday **23**

Be an encourager not a critic

Saturday **24**

The only day that really matters is today

Sunday **25**

Everyone has a unique point of view

**To succeed in life, you need
three things: a wishbone, a
backbone and a funny bone.**

Reba McEntire

October

In life, you have three choices:
Give up, Give in, or Give your all.

Charleton Parker

You have power over your mind,
Not outside events,
Realise this and you will find strength

Marcus Aurelis

Monday **26**	Full Moon, Hunter's Moon. October Bank Holiday

Don't confuse opinions with facts

Tuesday **27**	

Slow down, but don't stop

Wednesday **28**	

Seek to understand before being understood

Thursday **29**

Compassion and kindness work wonders

Friday **30**

Families are great training grounds

Saturday **31**

Fortune favours the brave

The privilege of a lifetime is to become who you truly are.
Carl Jung

Be kind whenever possible. It is always possible.
Dalai Lama

When you learn, teach. When you get, give.
Maya Angelou

Healthy Apple Crumble

What You Will Need

For the Crust and the Crumble

- 2 cups ground oats
- 5 tbsp coconut oil
- 4 tbsp water
- 2 tbsp honey or maple syrup (if vegan)

Filling

- 4 sweet apples, peeled and chopped
- 1 tbsp cinnamon
- 2 tbsp coconut oil

The How-To Part

1. Preheat the oven to 180C/ 350F.
2. Crust: Grind oats in your food processor. Add coconut oil, and honey/maple syrup if vegan and pulse. Add water 1 tbsp at a time and pulse again. The crust should be sticky and crumbly.
3. Cover the surface of a springform pan with coconut oil and pour 2/3 of the crust dough. Start pressing the dough from the middle to edges of the pan, working your way up with your fingers.
4. Filling: Chop your apples and saute them for 3-5 minutes at medium-high in a large non-stick pan with coconut oil and cinnamon. Let the filling cool off for 5 minutes and then spread it over the crust.
5. Using the rest of the dough, form crumbles with your fingers and put on top of the pie. Optionally you can also top your pie with pecans, walnuts or any other type of nuts. (Beware of people with Nut allergies).
6. Bake at 180C / 350 F for 20-30 minutes, until the crust becomes golden brown.
7. Let the pie cool off a bit and serve with your favourite toppings!

Bucket list for *November*

Resilience is knowing that you are the only one that has the power and the responsibility to pick yourself up.

Mary Holloway

I never dreamed about success. I worked for it.

Estée Lauder

November

I used to think I was indecisive, but now I'm not too sure.

Dave Chappelle

Each friend represents a world in us, a world possibly not born until they arrive, and it is only by this meeting that a new world is born.

Anaïs Nin

You are not here to make others understand you, you are here to understand yourself.

Kristen Butler

Live life as though nobody is watching, and express yourself as though everyone is listening.

Nelson Mandela

I'm the one that's got to die when it's time for me to die, so let me live my life the way I want to.

Jimi Hendrix

You can't really be present for the people in your life if you aren't taking care of yourself.

Kerry Washington

The saddest aspect of life right now is that science gathers knowledge faster than society gathers wisdom.

Isaac Asimov

Sunday **01**

Be flexible and flowing in the stream of life

It is more fun to talk with someone who doesn't use long, difficult words but rather short, easy words like "What about lunch?

A.A. Milne, Winnie-the-Pooh

November

I think Irish women are strong as horses, incredibly loyal and for the most part, funny, witty, bright and optimistic in the face of devastating reality.

Fionnula Flanagan

Monday **02**

Listen to your body's messages

Tuesday **03**

Conversation is an art, practice it

Wednesday **04**

Your intuition is always on your side

Thursday 05

Turn your problems into challenges

Friday 06

See the beauty within yourself

Saturday 07

You are allowed to make mistakes

Sunday 08

Declutter; make space for new things in your life

Doing nothing is hard, you never know when you're done.

Darynda Jones

November

Part of my act is meant to shake you up. It looks like I'm being funny, but I'm reminding you of other things. Life is tough, darling. Life is hard. And we better laugh at everything; otherwise, we're going down the tube.

Joan Rivers

Monday **09**	New Moon
	Self-expression is essential to life

Tuesday **10**	
	You are enough

Wednesday **11**	
	Do unto others as you would have others do unto you

Thursday **12**

Don't try and be a mind reader

Friday **13**

Parents only want the best for their children

Saturday **14**

Remember people's names

Sunday **15**

Smile when you answer the telephone

A business is simply an idea to make other people's lives better.

Richard Branson

November

The worst part of success is trying to find someone who is happy for you.

Bette Midler

I am not afraid of storms, for I am learning how to sail my ship.

Louisa May Alcott

Monday 16

Never send emails when you are upset

Tuesday 17

Decide what you want and take the steps to get you there

Wednesday 18

Don't fear what you don't understand

Thursday **19**

We can say anything to anyone at any time

Friday **20**

Courage and confidence come from within

Saturday **21**

All motivation is self-motivation

Sunday **22**

Let yourself be inspired

The best networking strategy is a helping others first strategy.

Nick Fox

November

Monday 23

The world is truly an amazing place

Tuesday 24   Full Moon, Beaver Moon

We all have our role to play

Wednesday 25

Set aside some quiet time

Thursday **26**

Play the game of life ... just for the fun of it

Friday **27**

Put an extra squeeze in your hugs today

Saturday **28**

You cannot fail but you can fail to try

Sunday **29**

The sweetest victories are shared

Death leaves a heartache no one can heal; love leaves a memory no one can steal.

From an Irish headstone

November

Listen to your favourite music

Easy Vegetable Stirfry

What You Will Need

- 2 tablespoons sunflower oil
- 4 spring onions (cut into 4cm lengths)
- 1 garlic clove (crushed)
- 1 cm fresh root ginger (peeled and grated)
- 1 carrot (cut into matchsticks)
- 1 red pepper (cut into thick matchsticks)
- 100 grams baby corn (halved)
- 1 courgette (cut into thick matchsticks)
- 150 grams mangetout (or sugar-snap peas, trimmed)
- 2 tablespoons hoisin sauce
- 2 tablespoons low-salt soy sauce

The How-To Part

1. Heat a wok on a high heat and add the sunflower oil. Add the spring onions, garlic, ginger and stir-fry for 1 minute, then reduce the heat. Take care to not brown the vegetables.
2. Add the carrot, red pepper and baby sweetcorn and stir-fry for 2 minutes. Add the courgette and sugar snap peas and stir-fry for a further 3 minutes. Toss the ingredients from the centre to the side of the wok using a wooden spatula. Do not overcrowd the wok and keep the ingredients moving.
3. Add 1 tablespoon water, hoisin and soy sauce and cook over a high heat for a further 2 minutes or until all the vegetables are cooked but not too soft. Serve with noodles or rice.

Bucket list for *December*

nges and
experience
and set
se it as
r, and m
tedly, b
s-believ
ations bu
kes you
caught
comes f
o matte
progress. Surround y
you, and never be

*The success of every woman should
be the inspiration to another.
We should raise each other up.*

Serena Williams

*Only I can change my life
No one can do it for me.*

Carol Burnett

December

Be careful not to misinterpret a situation.

Dance, even if you have nowhere to do it but your living room.

Mary Schmich

You miss 100% of the shots you don't take.

Wayne Gretzky

Tuesday 01

Start a Christmas list today

Wednesday 02

You are doing a great job

Thursday **03**

Today's food choices create tomorrow's health

Friday **04**

Time for a Christmas tree

Saturday **05**

Look for the win –win

Sunday **06**

Review your finances

The way you help heal the world is you start with your own family.
Mother Teresa

Your life belongs to you and you alone.
Anon

December

It takes 20 years to build a reputation and five minutes to ruin it. If you think about that, you'll do things differently.

Warren Buffett

You should set goals beyond your reach so you always have something to live for.

Ted Turner

Monday 07

Honour and value yourself

Tuesday 08

Be clear on your ground rules

Wednesday 09   New Moon

Accept the gift of acknowledgement

Thursday **10**

Keep your cool

Friday **11**

If you must, reprimand the behaviour but not the person

Saturday **12**

Listen to learn and understand

Sunday **13**

You are worthy of love

Be the woman who fixes another woman's crown without telling the world it was crooked.

Ami Morin

December

The hardest years in your life are those between ten and seventy.

Helen Hayes

When you know yourself you are empowered, when you accept yourself, you are invincible.

Tina Lifford

Monday **14**

Widen your circle of friends

Tuesday **15**

Plan a new adventure

Wednesday **16**

Rekindle an old friendship

Thursday **17**

Be the first to say 'sorry'

Friday **18**

Avoid the 'nay-sayers'

Saturday **19**

Be your own unsinkable ship

Sunday **20**

Do something special for a dear friend

Comfort is found among those who agree with you; growth among those who don't.

Frank A. Clark

December

Protect who is behind you and respect who is beside you.

Viking Saying

Believe you can and you're halfway there.

Theodore Roosevelt

Monday 21

Make a list of your best qualities and read it daily

Tuesday 22

Stay open and curious – it's all new

Wednesday 23

Two more sleeps

Cold Moon / Super Full Moon   Thursday **24**

Have you gotten everything for tomorrow

Christmas Day   Friday **25**

Celebrate Your Blessings

St. Stephen's Day   Saturday **26**

You make a difference

Sunday **27**

Give your left-over Christmas delights to the needy

**From home to home and heart to heart,
from one place to another. The warmth
and joy of Christmas bring us closer to each
other.**

Emily Matthews

December

Remember, Ginger Rogers did everything Fred Astaire did, but backwards and in high heels.

Faith Whittlesey

I have a confidence about my life that comes from standing tall on my own two feet.

Jane Fonda

Monday **28**

Focus on letting your inner beauty shine

Tuesday **29**

Be kind to all God's creatures

Wednesday **30**

Be clear and specific about what you want for 2027

*Your new year resolution can be
your health and well-being*

> *There are short-cuts to happiness,
> and dancing is one of them.*
>
> Vicki Baum

Chocolate Mousse

Dairy, Egg and Gluten Free – From Mama Rae

What You Will Need

- ½ can coconut cream
- ½ cup almond milk
- 3 tablespoons cacao powdered
- 3 tablespoons chia seeds
- 2 tablespoon maple syrup
- ½ teaspoon vanilla

The How-To Part

Add all ingredients to a bowl and whisk together. Pour into a serving dish. Chill until set – it will take about 2 ½ – 3 hours. Decorate with berries and shaved coconut.

Secrets From Mama Rae's Kitchen

You can turn this into a tart by making a crust of 1 cup of nuts, 1 cup of coconut, 4 medjool dates and ¼ cup of coconut oil. Process and put into a 20 cm tin. Chill till set and then pour mousse into base and return to the refrigerator for 3 hours or until set. Beautiful served with berries, chopped nuts, and shaved coconut. You can add 2-3 drops of peppermint or orange oil. Serve with fresh fruit or marinated orange or mandarin segments.

If you like it sweeter then add more maple syrup or whatever sweetener you are using.

NOTES

TO SEE OUR FULL RANGE OF DIARIES AND JOURNALS, PLEASE VISIT OUR WEBSITE:
www.getupandgodiary.com

CONTACT US

Get Up and Go
Publications
WE ASPIRE TO INSPIRE

Post: Get Up and Go Publications Ltd,
Unit 7A Cornhill Business Park, Ballyshannon,
Co Donegal, Ireland F94 H52
Email: info@getupandgodiary.com
Tel: 071 98 45938 or 085 1764297 (office hours)

ORDER FORM

The Irish Get Up and Go Diary (paperback), €12.95/£11 — Quantity ☐

The Irish Get Up and Go Diary (padded cover), €18.50/£16 — Quantity ☐

The Get Up and Go Diary (paperback), €12.95/£11 — Quantity ☐

Get Up and Go Diary for Busy Women (paperback), €12.95/£11 — Quantity ☐

Get Up and Go Diary for Busy Women (padded cover), €18.50/£16 — Quantity ☐

Get up and Go Young Person's Diary €12.95/£11 — Quantity ☐

Daily Guide to Good Health and Wellbeing (paperback), €16.50/£14 — Quantity ☐

Get Up and Go Gratitude Journal (padded cover), €18.50/£16 — Quantity ☐

Get Up and Go Wallplanner (size: A1), €4/£4 — Quantity ☐

Total number of copies ☐

ADD POSTAGE AND PACKING
Standard postage for 1/2 Paperback Diaries Anywhere in Ireland: €3.50
1 Paperback Diary To Great Britain & Europe: €5.95, USA/CAN: €9.50 Aus/NZ: €11.50
For bulk postage and tracking rates please refer to our website or call +353 85 1764297

I enclose cheque/postal order for (total amount including P+P):_____

Name: _____

Address: _____

Post Code: _____ Phone no: _____

Email:_____

**To pay by credit/debit card or with any other queries
please contact us 071 98 45938 or 085 1764297 during office hours**

NOTES

_____
_____
_____
_____
_____
_____
_____
_____
_____
_____
_____
_____
_____
_____
_____
_____
_____
_____
_____